How to use this book

This book is divided into three parts. The cover and centre colour pages form the castle. The black and white pages of figures, spooky and ghostly things are for you to pull out, colour in and cut out. The other colour pages, including this one, are full of supernatural facts, ghost stories as well as some creepy activities. There is a glossary on the inside back cover to help you to understand special spooky words.

Open the cover into a triangle. Fold the smaller flap over the book and push the castle tabs into the slots. Place on a flat surface.

Attach the side flaps to either side of the castle. Arrange the figures and spooky things in front of the castle.

Colour the pictures before cutting them out.

Fold the side flaps inwards to close the book.

Keep all the cut-outs in an envelope and tuck this into the book.

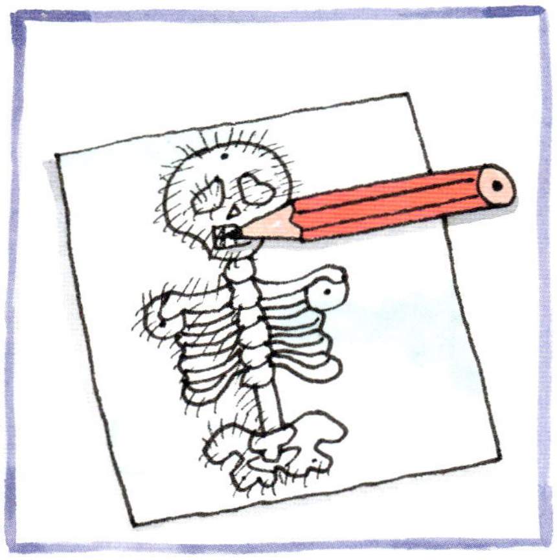

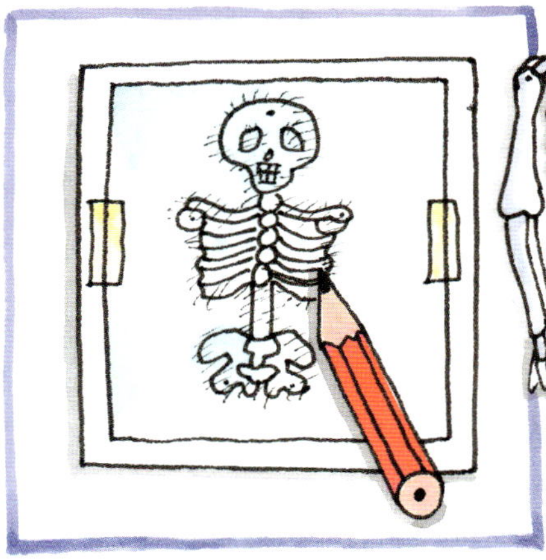

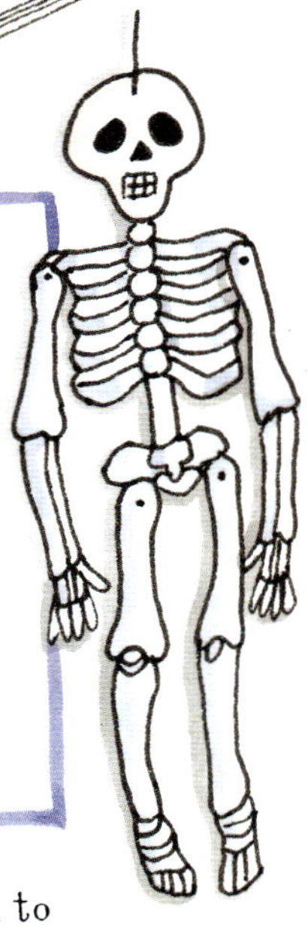

Tape a piece of tracing paper over the template or image. Trace in pencil.

Turn the tracing paper over and scribble over the lines with a pencil.

Turn over again and tape on to card or paper. Re-trace firmly over the lines. Remove the tracing paper.

Spooky castles

Ancient castles in Great Britain have a long history of violence and cruelty. Many are supposed to be haunted by the ghosts of those who suffered and died within their walls.

Ghostly Glamis

Glamis Castle, in Scotland, is meant to be the most haunted castle of all. In 1034, King Malcolm II of Scotland was killed there by a gang of rebels. Every year, on the day of his murder, his blood is said to appear on the floor of the room in which he died. His terrible screams can also be heard!

The rebels drowned trying to escape across a frozen loch (or lake). Some people believe that, on cold winter's nights, their ghosts still call for help over the icy water.

Dracula

Dracula is the most famous vampire story ever written. Count Dracula lived in a ruined castle, surrounded by jagged rocks, pine forests and wolves, in Transylvania (a region of Romania). At night he would change into a bat and hunt for victims so that he could drink their blood.

Freaky forest

Some castles are surrounded by dark, unfriendly forests. Here's how to make one, complete with spiders, bats and cobwebs.

Place some twigs in a large vase or jug. Pull cotton wool carefully until it is thin and web-like. Attach it to the ends of the twigs.

Following the instructions on the first page, trace the templates on to black paper and cut them out. Glue the bats or spiders on to the twigs and 'webs' or hang them on black thread.

TEMPLATES

Cotton wool 'webs'

The Haunted Castle

Once upon a time there was a king who lived in a castle high up in the mountains. All about there were pine forests where wild boar and deer lived. The king would go hunting and held great feasts and dances. The castle would be lit with a thousand lights and filled with the sound of laughter and music.

When the old king died his eldest son became king, as did his son after that. But times change and eventually the castle lay empty. The pine forests were cut down and people came to ski on the mountainsides. The castle was bought and turned into a smart hotel where skiers stayed in the winter and walkers in the summer.

The Haunted Castle

Colour, cut out and stand these pictures in front of the castle to tell the story.

1 The King hunting in the forest years ago.

2 Skiers

3 Guests leaving the hotel.

4 Ghost-hunters arriving at the hotel.

Colour the figures and other things and cut them out. Bend the flaps back along the dotted lines and stand the cut-outs up.

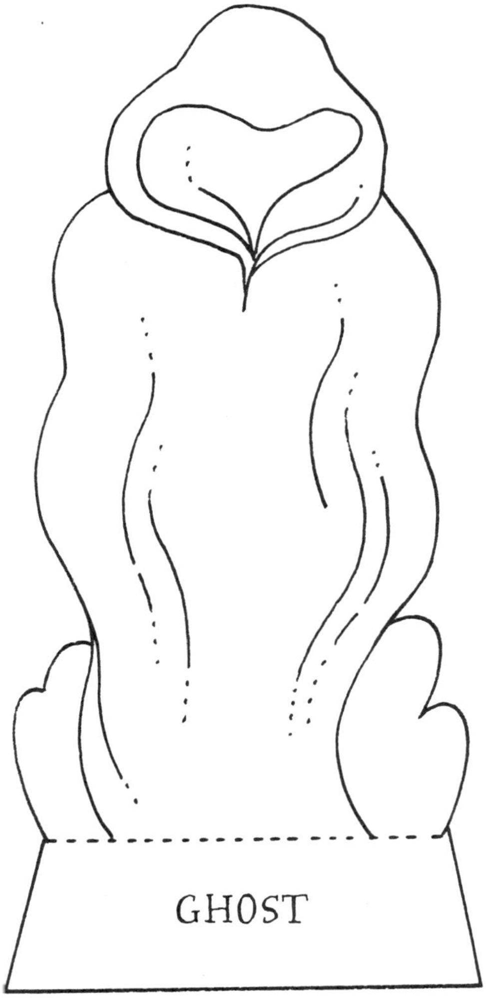

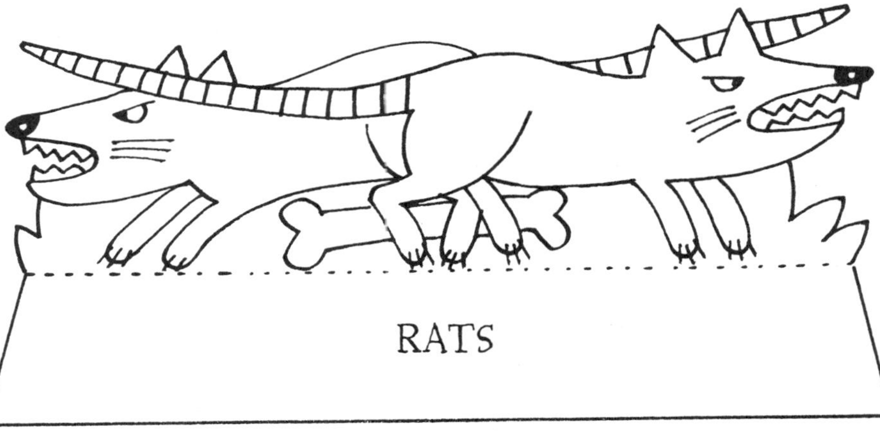

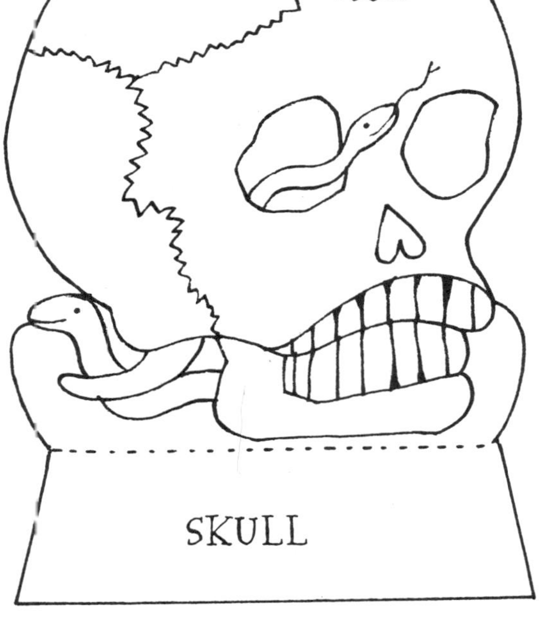

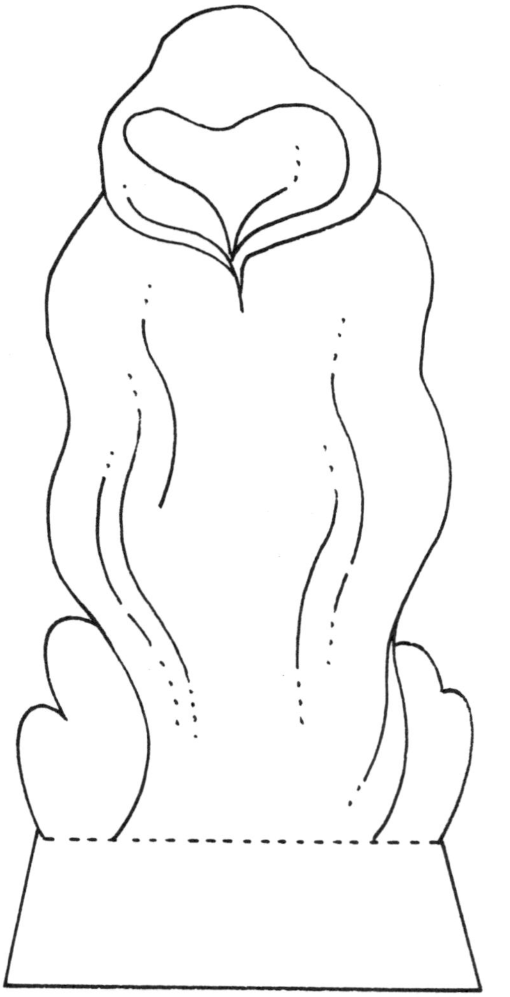

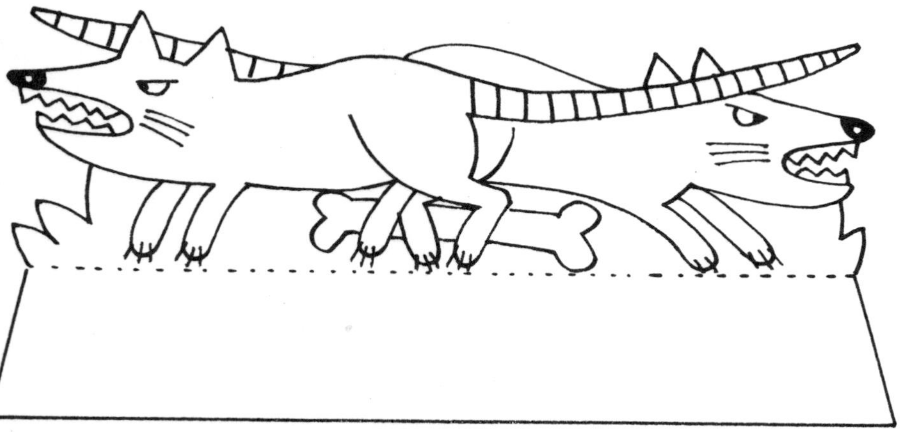

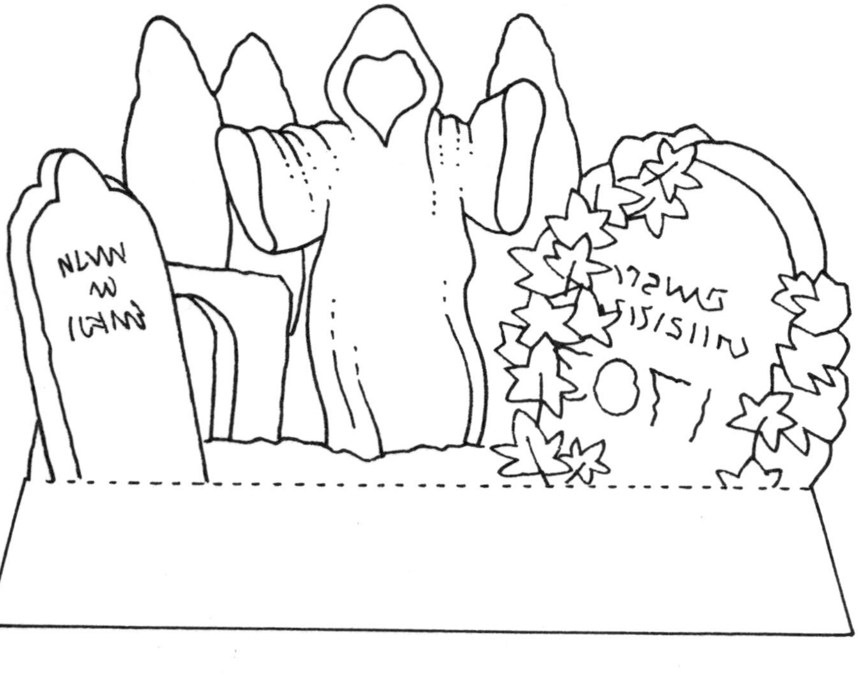

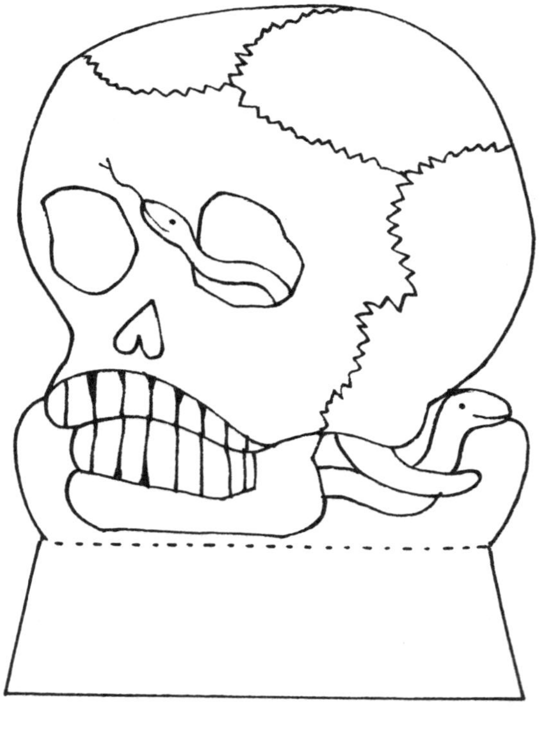

Stand the castle with the attached flaps on a flat surface. Arrange other cut-outs and figures around it.

CHURCHYARD

Bend back along the dotted line and stand it up.

Bend the flap forwards. Glue it on to the back of the right side of the castle.

TANGLE OF BRAMBLES

Bend back along the dotted line and stand them up.

Bend the flap forwards. Glue it on to the back of the left side of the castle.

PACK OF HOWLING WOLVES

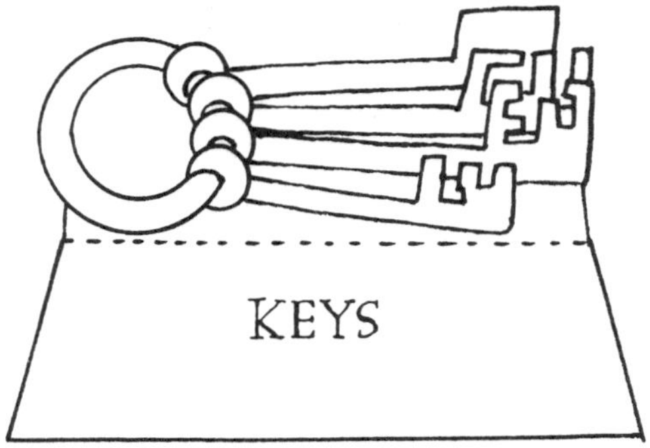
KEYS

CHAINED PRISONERS

SCARY TREE

VAMPIRE BATS

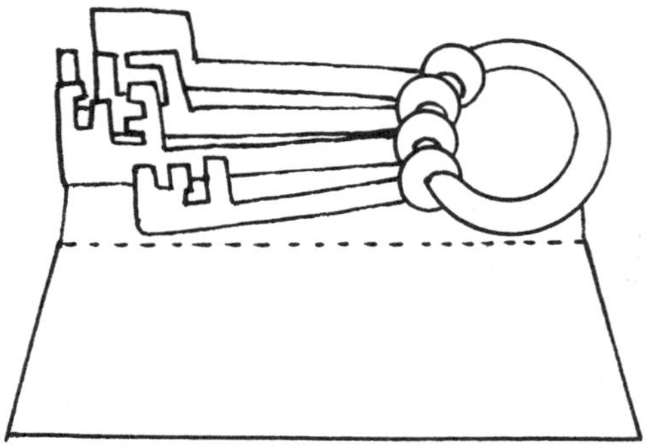

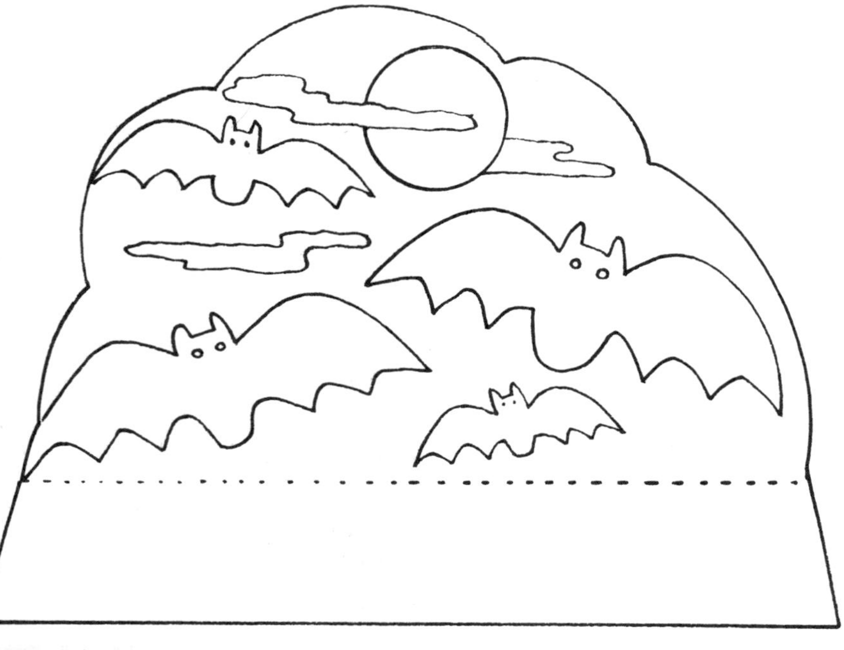

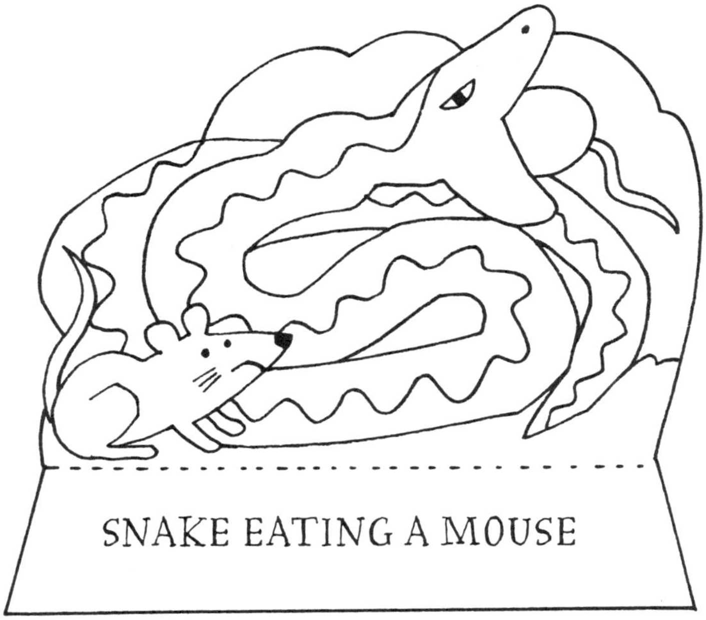
SNAKE EATING A MOUSE

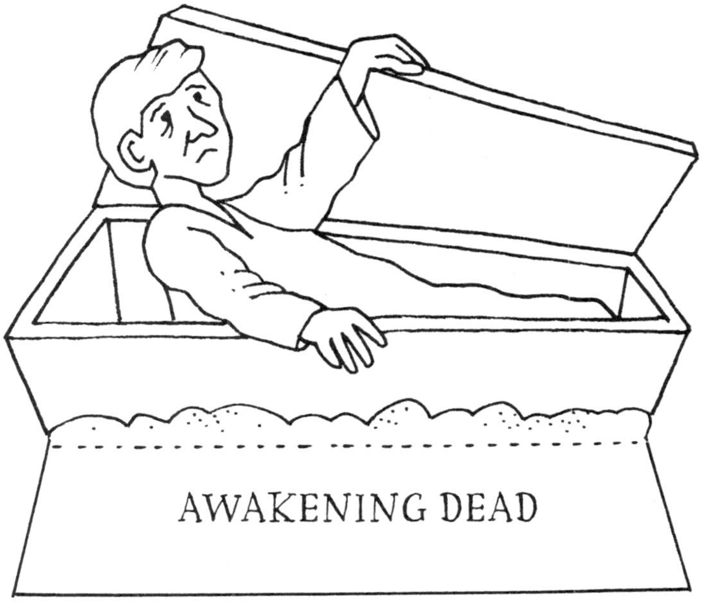
AWAKENING DEAD

DEADLY NIGHTSHADE

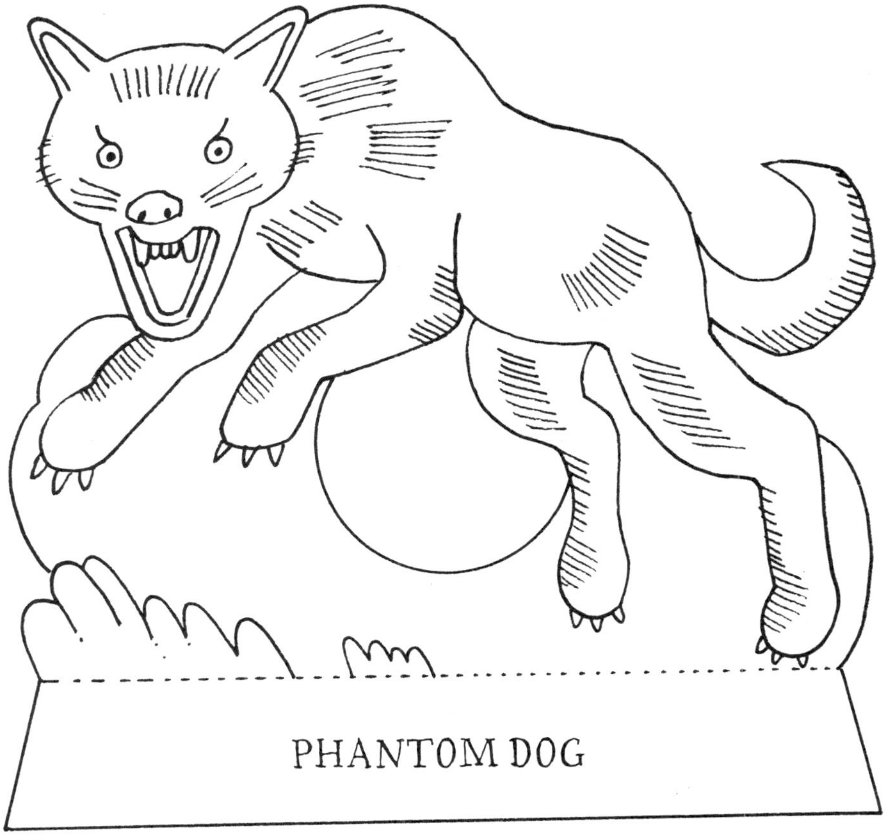
PHANTOM DOG

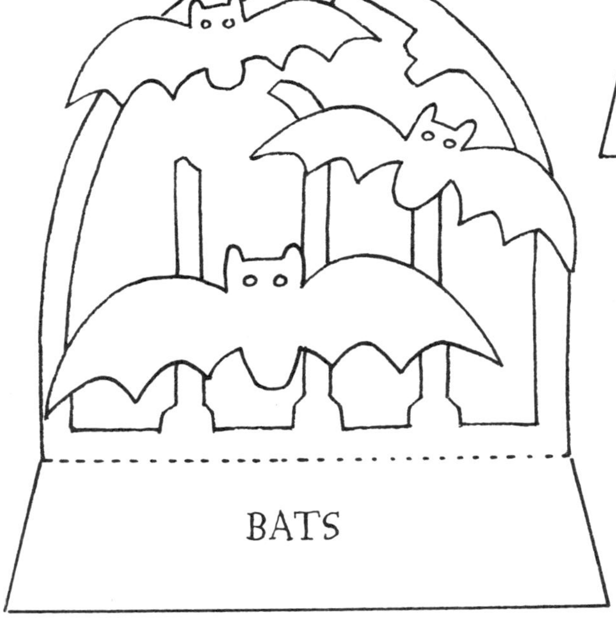
BATS

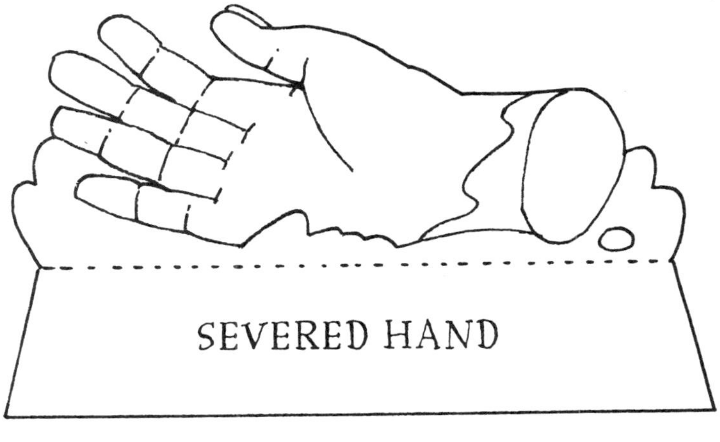
SEVERED HAND

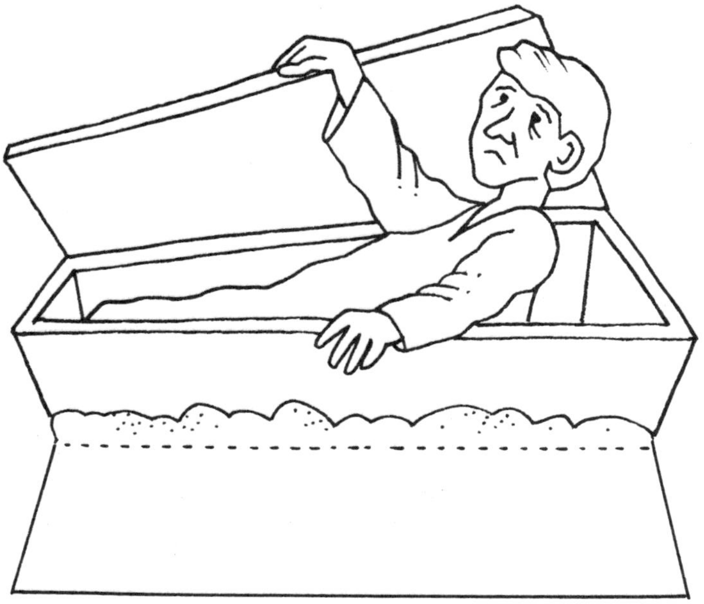
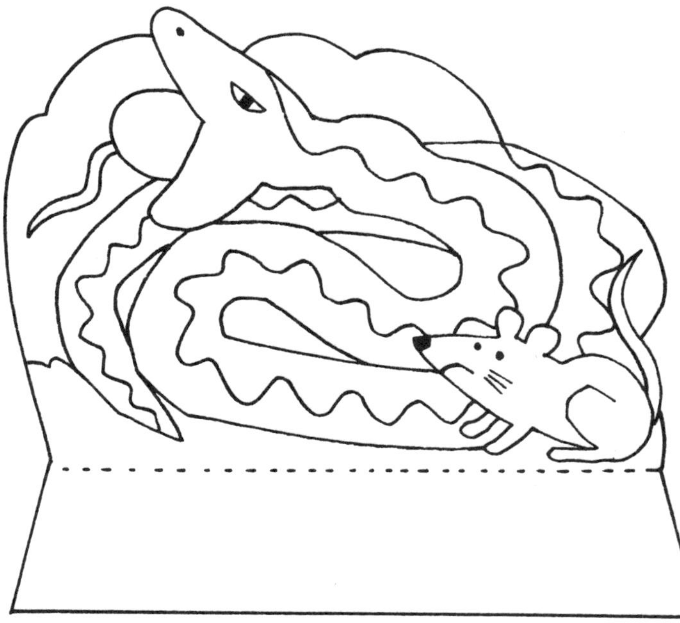

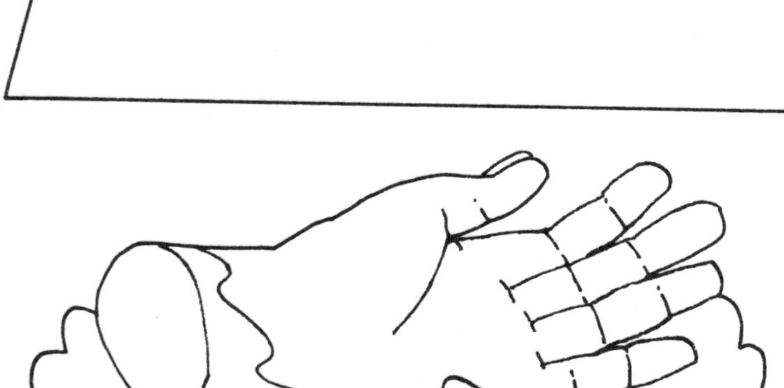

However, the ghosts of the king and his family had continued to live in their beloved castle and couldn't resist playing tricks on the guests. They would open the windows at night and let the snow blow in. They would change the channels on the TV and muddle all the shoes that had been left out for cleaning. They would even sometimes pull the bedclothes off them as they slept! People hated it and gradually stopped coming. The hotel had to close down.

A group of ghost-hunters decided to buy the hotel. They arranged special haunted weekends so that people who liked ghosts could come and see the king flitting down the corridors and the prince and princesses playing their tricks.

For these were happy ghosts who couldn't bear to leave the castle they had lived in so happily for so many years - EVER!

Ghosts and ghouls

Ghosts are the spirits of the dead. Some people think that they haunt the living because they were unhappy or were murdered. Most haunt the place in which they lived when they were alive. Many castles have their own resident ghosts.

Ghostly figures are often seen wearing the clothes they would have worn years ago, in their own time. Sometimes shadows or lights appear. Ghosts create an unsettling atmosphere, chills, smells or noises.

Many people do not believe in ghosts and the supernatural. They think that people are just imagining things. It's impossible to prove whether ghosts really exist or not, although many scientists have tried.

The most common animal ghost is a black dog.

In Mexico, on the 'Day of the Dead', people invite the spirits of dead friends and family to a party. They make decorations of skeletons and skulls.

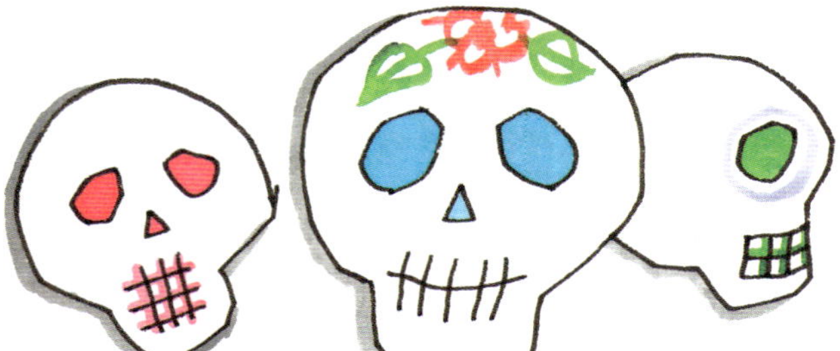

A poltergeist is a noisy angry spirit which throws things about and moves furniture!

Gloom and doom

The main colour to remember when dressing up for a spooky horror party is BLACK. Wear black clothes, black headgear and black accessories. Add some chains and a blue or purple streak in your hair and you'll give everyone the creeps!

Spooky jewellery

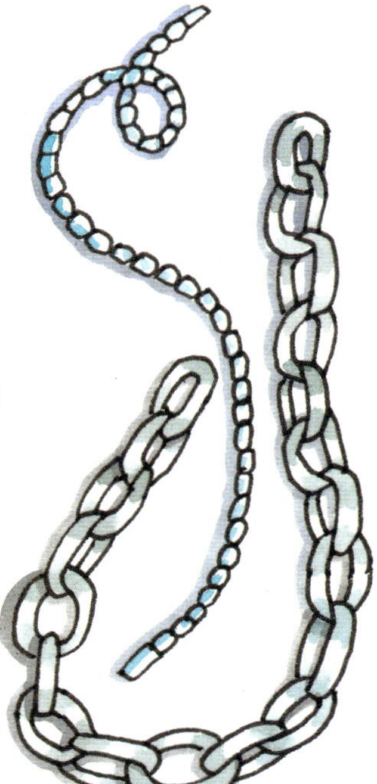

Make-up

White faces

Black eyes and mouth

Black or purple nail varnish

Chains

Hang silver chains on your jeans and wear them around your waist.

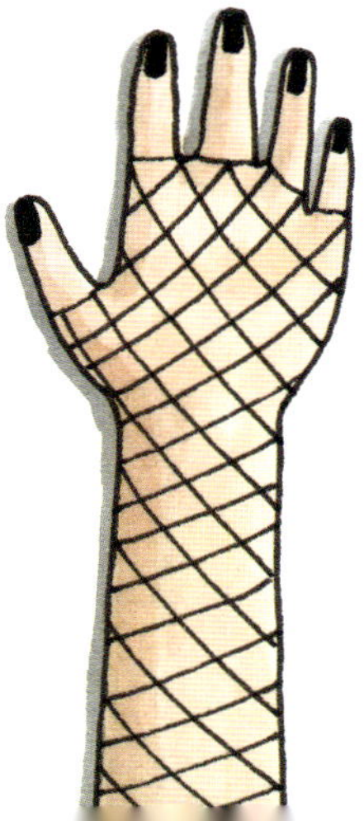

Clothes

Black trousers, T-shirts, skirts and tights. Black fishnet tights can be worn on your arms too!

Down in the dungeons

The word 'dungeon' comes from the French word 'donjon' meaning 'tower'. Most prisoners were kept in a castle's highest tower, guarded by soldiers. If lords and knights were kept for ransom, they were not treated too badly.

For most prisoners, though, life was grim. They had shackles placed around their ankles which were then attached to the wall. They could hardly move and just had mouldy bread and water to eat and drink.

Some castles had an 'oubliette' (from the French word for 'forgotten'). It was a dark, filthy, cylinder-shaped prison with no windows or doors. The prisoners were thrown in through a trapdoor at the top, never to see daylight again.